Our Constitutional Peril

Our Representation Abridged

by Bob Perry

Dorrance Publishing Co
585 Alpha Drive
Suite 103
Pittsburgh, PA 15238
Visit our website at *www.dorrancebookstore.com*

ISBN: 978-1-6461-0184-9
eISBN: 978-1-6461-0955-5

Dedication To:

Debra and Grant Nichols, owners and publishers of the weekly *Bradford Journal*, who have faithfully published my opinion column, which has been invaluable in the development of my thoughts and insights contained within this book.

All who contributed directly or indirectly in the founding the United States of America.

All who contributed directly or indirectly in the development of the Constitution of the United States of America, including the Framers of our Constitution—55 of whom were delegates to the Constitutional Convention.

Special Mention:
with some notes:

Abigail Adams: urged her husband, John Adams, to make the legal status of women equal to men when forming a new government. This was one of the earliest writings calling for women's equal rights.

John Adams, 2nd President: wrote "Defense of the Constitution of the Government of the United States of America."

Samuel Adams: helped to form resistance to the Stamp Act and played a vital role in organizing the Boston Tea Party.

Benjamin Franklin: one in the Committee of Five who drafted and presented to Congress that which became the Declaration of Independence.

Alexander Hamilton: author of the "Federalist Papers," advocating ratification of the Constitution.

John Hancock: president of the Second Continental Congress, at which agreement was made to form a Continental Army to be formed choosing George Washington to be its supreme commander.

Patrick Henry: fought hard for the ratification of the Constitution once the agreement was made to add a "bill of rights."

John Jay: drafted the first state's constitution for the state of New York.

Thomas Jefferson, 3rd President: wrote the Declaration of Independence.

Dolly Madison: held social functions in Washington and was pivotal in creating bipartisan cooperation in politics.

James Madison, 4th President: wrote the document that formed the model for the Constitution.

John Marshall: noted father of the American system of constitutional law.

George Mason: wanted the end of slave trade, fought for the inclusion of "the bill of rights" to become a signer of the Constitution.

James Monroe, 5th President: formed the Monroe Doctrine, ending European colonization in what was called the New World.

Thomas Paine: wrote "Common Sense," was a leader in the rebellion against British control during the American Revolution.

Betsy Ross: Upon the request of George Washington, Robert Morris, and George Ross, she sewed our first stars-and-stripes flag. This iconic American symbol leads parades and symbolizes all that is good in our sovereign nation.

Mercy Otis Warren: the first significant woman historian who wrote an eyewitness account of the American Revolution.

George Washington, 1st President: proceeded over the Constitutional Convention, led military forces to victory in our War of Independence.

Contents

Author's Note

The perception that I present in this book declares that our Constitution has been ***ABRIDGED*** is ***ABSOLUTE*** and it is ***Our Constitutional Peril***. This is an ultimate ***Constitutional Crisis*** created by representatives in their own interests but lacking insight into the perception I address and putting our Freedom and Democracy in Peril. The contents of this book are my insights, thoughts and suggestions with the hope that with recognition as to the truths result in efforts being put forth to address and rectify the unfortunate reality that we have not lived up to our Founders' Vision. To continue on this present course ***Our Constitutional Peril*** will irrevocably alter our Democratic Republic, leading us into further chaos and possible revolution and tyranny.

The vision of the Framers of our Constitution has not been fulfilled as the misunderstandings, misinterpretations, and misapplications of our Constitution, and in particular our "Form of Government," has led us to a government disproportionately influenced by wealth, the elite, and those holding power. We have realized the very thing our Founders attempted to avoid.

This book (a work in progress) is my declaration that our "Form of Government" that has evolved is unconstitutional as the "Representational Relationship" (our "Form of Government") established through the Constitutional electoral process has been diminished (**ABRIDGED**).

Some of the important points being made will appear in various chapters as they are applicable in those chapters.

PROLOGUE

The purpose of this book is to identify what has been overlooked in the interpretation and application of our Constitution, along with suggested changes which, if applied, would reestablish the vision and intent of our Founders. This book will revive the spirit, vision, and intent of our Founders in creating and establishing our Constitutional Democratic Republic. The process of creating our Constitution was very deliberative using the comparisons of previous governments of the world and resulted in creating a "Form of Government," which, if understood and applied as intended, would endure throughout time. Due to the misunderstandings, misinterpretations, and misapplications of our Constitution there are ongoing attempts to replace our "Form of Government," which will inevitably lead to some form of tyranny. The chapters of the book will provide my perception of our Founders' intent in establishing a "Form of Government," which needed to be and remain *sacrosanct*. If understood, my perception will effectually change much of existing law as it pertains to Campaign Finance, which will have the results of fulfilling our Founders' Vision.

Our Founders' Vision

Our Founders' vision was simple—to create a government based upon and guided by a Constitution, which would establish a Republic designed to provide fair democratic representation with an overriding goal of avoiding such representation to be disproportionately influenced by wealth, the elite, and those holding power.

Our Form of Government

Identifying our "Form of Government" has been somewhat nonspecific and confusing, but herein I identify it specifically giving it clarity, noted importance, and state the need for it to be and remain ***sacrosanct***.

When establishing any government it is paramount that the form be specific and it must be adhered to and remain ***sacrosanct***, free from any change or interference. A "Form of Government" is akin to a mission statement accompanied with bylaws necessary for any organization to adhere to for survival. Our "Form of Government's" mission is to ensure implementation and guarantee success of our Founders' Vision.

Understanding and applying the "Form of Government" as envisioned by our Founders is the "heart of the matter" of this book.

Our Democratic Republic's "Form of Government," as established in our Constitution, is representational and is specifically the "Representational Relationship" between constituents and elected representatives as established through the electoral process. Intended was the formation of an alliance between individual constituents and representatives with the representatives having and fulfilling the fiduciary duty with their constituents.

The "Representational Relationship" was of special concern by our Founders as they hoped the "Relationship" would be fair. To be "fair," the "Relationship" is required to be *sacrosanct* and, as noted, free from any change or interference.

To be fair as well as *sacrosanct* our "Form of Government" also needed to be from inception **UNABRIDGED**: unaffected by any interpretation of the Bill of Rights; any legislative enactment; any governing fiat; judicial opinions and rulings, any judicial analytic (synthetic or evaluative judgment); any interpretation variance of our Constitution; any additional "Representational Relationships."

Our Bill of Rights was added to the original drafting of our Constitution so as to appease some who needed more to support it and this inclusion solidified its approval, but, the adding of these Rights were obviously never intended to interfere with the establishment of or violate the *sacrosanctity* of our "Form of Government." Unfortunately, as our political world has evolved, our "Form of Government" has not been held sacrosanct. It has been adversely and unconstitutionally affected by other considerations, including but not limited to interpretations of our Bill of Rights, legislative enactments, governing fiats, judicial rulings, judicial analytics (both synthetic and evaluative judgments), and other interpretative variances of the Constitution which have permitted the adding of additional "Representational Relationships." In holding our "Form of Government" as being *sacrosanct*, nothing else can be given equal weight, as when something is given equal weight, our "Form of Government" is altered; thus diminished (**ABRIDGED**). Indeed this is *Our Constitutional Peril*!

The "Form of Government" that has evolved is not that that which our Founders envisioned and in their wisdom they made provision for the citizens to amend our Constitution as needed or desired, but shortcuts have been made resulting in major compromises shredding original intent which is leading us to failure. Unamended changes made has trampled on the "Right of the People" for their consultation and approval.

The following chapter on "Representational Relationship" explains in detail the components that are necessary to assure implementation and success of our Founders' Vision, which, if held ***sacrosanct***, protects against the possibility of tyranny.

Representational Relationship

As described in the "Our Form of Government" Chapter, the "Representational Relationship" between elected representatives and their constituents is truly our "Form of Government" and it was to be and remain *sacrosanct*. Representation of constituents is a fiduciary duty holding the trust and interests of constituents individually and collectively above the interests of all others, including any other entity, individual, group, organization, or political party. Representative candidates and elected representatives are to be the "people's candidates" without interference from all non-constituents. The power of representation emanates from individual constituents through the electoral process and representation belongs to them. The establishment of any additional "Representational Relationship" adds others to whom the representative becomes answerable to does mititate (influence and diminish) the fiduciary responsibility to the individual constituents.

Clearly as our political world has evolved our "Form of Government" has been ***ABRIDGED*** reflected in the verifiable diminishing of the intended "Representational Relationship" between constituents and representatives. What is needed is to reconnect representatives and connect representative candidates with constituents in order to develop the "Representational Relationship" as envisioned by our Founders. Our Founders we most concerned that the representation between representatives and constituents be fair and to accomplish this there are three dependency components needed in order to avoid the disproportionate influenced by wealth, the elite and those holding power:

(1) the dependency of the representative candidate upon constituents for votes to gain or retain office through the electoral process. The elected candidate is to be the "people's candidate."

(2) the dependency of the constituents upon representatives to fulfill their fiduciary duty; hold their trust and interests plus being answerable directly to them. It is inherent on the part of representatives to interact continually with their constituents to be current and knowledgeable of the their interests and will.

(3) the dependency of representative candidates upon individual constituents for the exclusive fiscal support in seeking office. Contributions received by a candidate are deemed to be for funding the candidate's election alone and not transferable. Contributions are necessarily to be personal resources and not from any other source, identifiable and subject to verification.

This, as a requirement, serves to connect the individual constituents with the representatives and representative candidates promoting confidence in the representation being offered and a sense of responsibility on the part of the representatives and representative candidates to understand and execute the required fiduciary duty that comes with holding an elected office.

This, as a requirement, encourages constituents to become engaged, increases support, and builds trust as their interests are recognized and honored.

This, as a requirement, also serves to isolate and protect the representatives and representative candidates from being disproportionately influenced by wealth, the elite, and those holding power as envisioned by our Founders. Representatives in particular necessarily need to be isolated from the pressures exerted from donors through the expectancy of returning favors and retribution for not fulfilling requests for favors, etc.

This, as a requirement, would create a reasonable playing field that will likely eliminate the need to establish term limits; for legislative representatives in particular. Political parties favor the Campaign Finance Laws as they are as they all but guarantee most representatives will be reelected, which gives the parties more control and power over the representatives but at the same time it diminishes the ability of constituents of being successful in challenging to replace the representatives. The Laws must change!

The permitting of contributing to the campaign of a representative or representative candidate initiates a relationship invite from the contributor and likely a relationship acceptance from the candidate.

Once a contributor gives a contribution the representative or representative candidate is drawn back to soliciting and accepting additional contributions from that contributor. The contributor becomes eager to donate additional funds when the representative is responsive to the interests and requests of the contributor for special consideration. When a contributor who is not an individual constituent donates contributions and establishes a "Representational Relationship" with a representative or representative candidate the resulting "Representational Relationship" with the individual constituent becomes diminished.

Each individual constituent must have equal weight when it comes to representation and since contributions by other than individual constituents affects the scale of representation contributions need be limited to individual constituents. Influence from other than individual constituents does create unequal weighted influence.

"Representational Relationships" that are created by other than individual constituents creates major problems for representatives in all levels of government especially in legislative efforts in the creation of laws. Special interest groups are a major problem as they are permitted to contribute campaign funding to a representative or representative candidate which without question creates an invite for a relationship which can provide access, special representation and special consideration for creating desired legislation, voting for on such legislation or voting in opposition on such legislation. Reportedly, Special Interest contributions make up the major funding for representatives and representative candidates which provides clear proof that said contributions do diminish (**ABRIDGE**) "Representational Relationships."

It is clear that the "Representational Relationship" has needed to be interdependent with the representative candidates and representatives depending solely upon individual constituents to provide the votes and campaign funding in securing the desired offices and the elected representatives providing undiminished representation for the constituents.

Read "Special Interests" chapter as it makes clear who are the "Special Interests" and insights into the power they have in our government.

Our Nation of Laws

We are truly a Nation of Laws as designed with three equal branches of government and as our political world has evolved shortcomings which are adversely affecting the "Representational Relationship" between representatives and constituents. Laws created which permit a disproportionate influence from the wealthy, the elite, and those holding power is without question unconstitutional. The Campaign Finance Laws which have been created and upheld include provisions which permit the influence and the Laws' constitutionality must be challenged and found unconstitutional.

Legislative Branch:

Legislators take an oath of office to uphold, support, and defend our Constitution. To uphold the Constitution it is inherent upon each legislator to read, understand, and determine the constitutionality of each bill prior to voting on each bill. To be constitutional, it is imperative for legislative rules to provide the opportunity and the time for each legislator to make the noted consideration and determination of constitutionality. Our Constitution provides our legislatures the right to create their own rules but it is abundantly clear that some of the rules fall short of being democratic thus not supporting and upholding our Constitution. Any legislator who holds and practices the attitude of not being concerned about the constitutionality of a bill as "it can be challenged later" is failing in fulfilling their "Oath of Office." While the Judicial branch does have the responsibility of determining if a law is constitutional or not, the determination is a requirement upon a court challenge, not as a routine consideration on all laws enacted. It is a responsibility of each representative involved in the creation of, enactment of and adjudication of laws to question the constitutionality of laws under consideration. Failure for the legislative rules to provide the opportunity for each legislator to fulfill their "Oath of Office" is undoubtedly unconstitutional. A suggestion would be that the legislative rules include a mandated "Constitutionality Vote" to confirm each legislator has completed the individual consideration and determination prior to any vote on final approval of the bill. This is especially true as last minute additions and revisions inclusive of "earmarks" and revisions often change the funding, composition, and possibly constitutionality of the bill. Clearly, a constitutionality check would support our Founders' vision as they never intended the rules the legislature would write would include some which interfere with legislators' ability to provide the best representation.

Undemocratic is unconstitutional. Legislatures are quite dysfunctional, in a large part, due to questionable legislative rules and procedures. Legislative bills need to be valued upon and voted upon the content and merit exclusive of any disproportionate outside influence. Legislators all must also be isolated from any disproportionate outside influence, especially Special Interests. The Senate is of special concern as rules permit the leadership there to table bills which find their way there denying fair consideration to move forward to be debated and voted on.

Consideration of the voting process reveals in reality bills being voted on all too often do not receive the fiduciary consideration of the legislators' constituents first and foremost due to the pressures exerted by outside interests inclusive of the party affiliations and the fact the voting record is open for inspection and reported on. To be able to overcome the influences and permit the representatives to fulfill their fiduciary duty it may be necessary for voting (in some if not all instances) to become only a fact each legislator voted but not how. Clearly the recording of each vote cast does place limits upon the representative to vote in certain ways so as to assure an outcome of the vote which in turn does diminish our "Form of Government." A challenge is necessary to determine if the vote recording of how one voted is constitutional or not as it does show some limitations on how one votes.

It goes without saying, well it should be, but to fulfill the vision of our Founders, legislators individually must protect the creation and passing of bills to become law from allowing such laws to be disproportionately influenced by wealth, the elite and those holding power. The influence has been, is, and will continue to be prevalent unless and until the influence in the form of campaign contributions is limited to come solely from individual constituents they represent as they are deserving of the undiminished (*UN-ABRIDGED*) representation.

Executive Branch:

Executives, who sign approved bills into law, also take an oath of office to uphold, support, and defend our Constitution and are no less responsible than legislators to read, understand, and determine the constitutionality of each bill prior to signing each bill into law.

Taking the implied surety that the bill is constitutional and in the best interests of the constituents does not fulfill the elected representative's individual fiduciary responsibility of assuring both conditions are true. Once a law is enacted the executive is responsible for directing all appropriate agencies that the new law is enforced. Clearly this is not always the case.

Judicial Branch:

In determining the constitutionality of any law the judiciary considers if any precedent exists which provides a basis for an opinion and a determination. Any law which is considered "settled law" leaves little wiggle room for a reversal in an interpretational change, but, in light of the perception I present in this book, review and serious consideration for changes in Campaign Finance Laws is warranted. Properly considered and properly determined all laws which permit the disproportionate influence from the wealthy, the elite and those holding power will be declared unconstitutional. The Judiciary, which constitutionally cannot make law, should instruct the appropriate legislatures to revise the Campaign Finance Laws to include the isolation of representatives and representative candidates from the noted disproportionate influences.

Campaign Finance

It is specifically and without question our Campaign Finance Laws have permitted our political system to evolve to where our representatives have become disproportionately influenced by wealth, the elite and those holding power. The Laws have created ***Our Constitutional Peril*** by ***ABRIDGING*** (diminishing) our "Form of Government." The Laws must be revised to insure our Founders' Vision will be reestablished.

There is undoubtedly too much money in politics and while financial support of representative candidates and representatives do require support in seeking election into and retaining the office they desire, there needs to be a way to eliminate most of the funds which are disproportionately influencing legislation, governance, and judicial activity.

As stated in Chapter One, Our Founders' vision was simple—to create a government based upon and guided by a Constitution which would establish a Republic designed to provide fair democratic representation with an overriding goal of avoiding such representation to be disproportionately influenced by wealth, the elite and those holding power.

Holding to this vision, I looked at the creation of our "Form of Government" as separate from any other part of our Constitution and considered it like a "mission statement," necessary for any organization to follow in order to be successful. The necessary element required to avoid the disproportionate influence of the wealthy, the elite, and those holding power is isolating representatives and representative candidates from receiving any funds directly or indirectly at any time from other than individual constituents. Inappropriate funding does produce disproportionate influences in legislation that is created, legislation that is thwarted, enactments of laws, enforcement of laws, and adjudication of laws. All would find improvement with the removal of inappropriate funding as I am proposing.

Current Campaign Finance Laws permit multiple ways for solicitation and the receiving of funds but the permitting of multiple ways to contribute gives the elites, wealthy and those in power a disproportionate advantage by which to invite the creation of additional "Representational Relationships" not created through the electoral process. Multiple ways creates a targeted focus on representatives in particular to seek repeated funds from big donors which further diminishes the "Representational Relationship" between representatives and constituents. The revision of Campaign Finance laws to correct the improper flow of funds will not eliminate "bag money" from influence seekers finding its way into the hands of representatives and representative candidates, their relatives or associates, but, increased penalties would be recommended for anyone violating new laws. "Dark money" will have a more difficult time finding its way into a candidate's funds as the revision suggested herein requires the identification of all donors which gives the opportunity for contributions to be verified.

As noted before, anything which diminishes (ABRIDGES) the "Representational Relationship" is unconstitutional and it is a fact that contributions solicited by and accepted by representative candidates and representatives from non-constituents creates a weighted influence and reduces the dependency upon constituents for funding and increases "Representational Relationships" with non-constituents. History proves that representatives do represent donors in their seeking favorable support for causes overshadowing the interests and desires of constituents.

Going further, contributions from groups of constituents also has the same effect as the "Representatinal Relationship" for the individual constituent is diminished in favor of the groups.

It is the individual constituents who elect representatives and it is the individual constituents who has a rightful claim for the "Representational Relationship."

This leaves us with only one possible solution to eliminate most of the funds which are disproportionately influencing legislation, governing, and judicial activity that being for all campaign funds accepted by a representative or representative candidate must come from individual constituents.

In summary: For our "Form of Government," to be effective and constitutional, there are three components of dependency that necessarily make up the "Representational Relationship" alliance:

(1) the dependency of the representative candidate upon constituents for votes to gain or retain office through the electoral process. The elected candidate is to be the "people's candidate."

(2) the dependency of the constituents upon elected representatives to fulfill their fiduciary duty; hold their trust and interests plus being answerable directly to them. It is inherent on the part of representatives to interact continually with their constituents to be current and knowledgeable of the their interests and will.

(3) the dependency of representative candidates upon individual constituents for the exclusive fiscal support in seeking office. Contributions received by a candidate are deemed to be for funding the candidate's election alone and not transferable. Contributions are necessarily to be personal resources and not from any other source, identifiable and subject to verification.

Virtually every representative and representative candidate has violated our Constitution even though they have lived to existing Campaign Finance Laws as the Laws do contain provisions which are clearly unconstitutional

To become constitutional, Campaign Finance Laws require revisions be made to isolate representatives and representative candidates from being enticed to provide "Representational Relationships" to other than the individual constituents.

It has been reported that less than 10% of campaign funds come from constituents which makes it easy to draw the conclusion that "Representational Relationships" created outside the constituent base are common and as stated before, this does in fact diminish (ABIRDGE) our "Form of Government."

Each election cycle, which includes the primary and general election, needs to stand upon its own as far as campaign contributions and expenses are concerned with a recommendation there be no carry over to the next election cycle as part of a "war chest" which gives an advantage over challenging candidates. Funds collected and not expensed in no way should be used to enrich any candidate, any other candidate, any family member, or other associates. Funds need to be dissolved in some feasible way within a reasonable time period so as not to conflict with any succeeding election cycle.

The Federal Elections Committee (FEC) should review this information and formulate the way forward to revise Finance Laws and regulations making them constitutional.

What is needed to reconnect representatives and representative candidates to reestablish the necessary dependency relationships forming the alliance needed to fulfill our Founders' Vision.

History proves that representatives do represent donors in their seeking favorable support for causes overshadowing the interests and desires of constituents.

There is a question as to Campaign Finance limits on donations to a representative or a representative candidate and constitutionally I perceive there is but one limit that can be argued as legitimate and that is limiting contributions solely from individual constituents. As to any limit on the amount one can give I perceive there arguably must be no limit. Remembering our Founders' Vision to have representation void of being disproportionately influenced by wealth, the elite and those holding power, contributions by individual constituents keeps the influence limited to the very people being represented. Making contributions public information will reveal how much anyone contributes will educate the constituency of any disproportionate influence is being sought and will affect selections on just who to vote for or not. All contributions necessarily need to be verifiable which will require the identification of the individual along with their address and the funds contributed cannot be from a third party.

So who to vote for are candidates who seek and accept contributions from individual constituents in combination of self-funding by candidates. Be wary of any candidate who only self-funds as their agenda may be theirs alone and not be in the best interests of the constituency. I am hoping this effort will energize and engage the constituency to become more invested and engaged in supporting and electing qualified candidates irrespective of party affiliation as they will realize better and more effective representation.

Special Interest

A Special Interest in politics is any entity or group of entities other than an individual constituent who seeks to establish a "Representational Relationship" with a representative candidate or representative in order to acquire access and special consideration. Included in the ways to gain access, consideration, and influence is the ability by law to make campaign contributions. The point of this writing is to assert that all laws created which permit Special Interests who are not individual constituents to make contributions to representatives and/or representative candidates adversely affects the ability of representatives to honor their fiduciary duty to constituents by placing their interests and concerns before those of constituents. Whenever a fiduciary duty is adversely effected then the cause has diminished the "Representational Relationship" and is unquestionably unconstitutional. It is appropriate for a representative candidate or representative to consider supporting and representing worthwhile ideas put forth by any Special Interest but it is not appropriate to establish a "Representational Relationship" with any non-constituent Special Interest.

Identifying Special Interests will shed some light into the corruptive forces representatives are faced with as they attempt to fulfill their responsibilities and somehow honor their "Oath of Office."

I must start off with the number-one Special Interest which is often a political party. Be it the Democratic Party, the Republican Party, or any other, a political party wants and demands allegiance in exchange for the support in gaining and regaining office along with committee assignments. This is real power which disproportionately influences the "Representational Relationship" with constituents. By accepting contributions from a party a representative faces coercion whenever the leadership of the party expresses a desired outcome. Whenever the best interests of the representative's constituents is overridden by the Special Interest of a party, then the permission, by law, for a party to make contributions is unconstitutional. And so it goes for all other non-constituent Special Interest: must be denied to isolate all representatives from being disproportionately influenced.

Making a list of all Special Interests is unnecessary as the list changes constantly, so it suffices to say, for the purposes of making campaign contributions, any entity other than an individual constituent attempting or making a contribution is considered a Special Interest. Special Interests are in the business of seeking, requesting, and even commanding influence in each branch of our government and permitting it to continue is destroying our Republic. Among those who would not be able to contribute are relatives of a representative candidate or representative if they are not a constituent.

Oath of Office

Any representative, elected or appointed, who has not read and understood our Constitution and does not uphold, support and defend it violates their "Oath of Office' AND does not belong serving in government.

Virtually every elected representative has not lived up to their "Oath of Office" as described below:

Legislators, in order to uphold, support, and defend the Constitution of the United States, must come to understand that it is an individual responsibility to read, understand, and consider the constitutionality of each and every bill they are to vote upon. Legislatures, in fulfilling their constitutional right to write their own rules, are writing some rules which appear not to be democratic as they do not always provide the opportunity for legislators to read, understand, and consider the constitutionality of each bill being put forth for voting on. It is inherent for each legislator to insist that the opportunity stated be included in the legislative rules. Legislative rules necessarily have a duty to poll voting members prior to a vote to address and resolve any issue found to be cited as unconstitutional. Legislators are elected to represent constituents and need the opportunity stated in order to fulfill their fiduciary duty to constituents first before consideration of political affiliation, Special Interest and all others. As an individual responsibility legislators must each determine constitutionality and never accept the word of anyone else including another legislator, an associate, or a committee.

Executives, in order to uphold, support, and defend the Constitution of the United States, must come to understand that it is an individual responsibility to read, understand, and consider the constitutionality of each and every bill they are to sign into law and enforcing said law. Executives necessarily have a duty to address any issue found to be unconstitutional and return the bill to the legislature for revision or veto the bill citing the unconstitutional issue.

The Judiciary, in order to uphold, support, and defend the Constitution of the United States, in deliberating the constitutionality of an issue or law presented before them must understand they are not to create law by their opinions but respond with direction to the appropriate legislature to revise the law to become constitutional or strike the law down. This is especially true of the Supreme Court who has final say on constitutionality. To be fair and clear of bias, at least perceptually, the judge panel reviewing the issue or law at hand should comprise of no less than three judges. Putting a stay on an Executive Order as well as existing law needs fair and unbiased support for any stay.

Free Speech

The ability to speak one's mind in a place and way of one's choosing is without doubt a cherished Right we all enjoy.

In support of a representative or a representative candidate anyone, citizen or not, has a free speech right by any means which does not create a weighted imbalance. Speech is expressed in many ways and expressing support for a representative candidate or representative by the utilization of numerous ways including, but not limited to; newspapers, television, social media, letters (both written and in Braille), polls, benefits, rallies, parades, posters, advertisements, phone calls, door-to-door visitations, audio, video, print of all sorts, and gesture.

Using and justifying anything that is tangible, such as campaign contributions of money or in-kind contributions, as being an expression of Free Speech does not equate with speech which is an intangible. Campaign contributions can and often does create a weighted imbalance when the contributions come from the wealthy, elite, or those in power when they are not individual constituents of the representative or the representative candidate.

We can cite money to explain by recognizing money is taxable while Free Speech is not.

Cease taxing and regulating the flow of money and there might be an argument to the contrary.

When addressing representative candidates and representatives, anyone, constituent or not, can use of Free Speech in order to convey interests, beliefs, opinions, suggestive ideas, support, and endorsement or not. One's vote can be viewed as an expression of Free Speech but is limited by the electoral process to only those who are eligible constituents who are citizens.

What's Unconstitutional

Here are some issues I perceive as being unconstitutional:

- It is unconstitutional to interpret our Constitution by giving different meanings to the words as written.
- It is unconstitutional to not respect and hold our Constitution as being ***sacrosanct***.
- It is unconstitutional to ***ABRIDGE*** (diminish) our "Form of Government" in any way.
- It is unconstitutional to not amend our Constitution when the need is created by changing a provision or adding a provision to properly give authority under our Constitution.
- It is unconstitutional to make federal law reserved for the states.
- It is unconstitutional to abdicate any responsibility assigned by the Constitution to another branch of the government or authority.
- It is unconstitutional to establish any statute which in effect can create additional "Representational Relationships" not established through the electoral process.

- It is unconstitutional for the judiciary to declare any statute constitutional which in effect can create an additional "Representational Relationship" not established through the electoral process.

- It is unconstitutional for legislative representatives to vote on any bill before each representative is provided the opportunity to read, understand, make a determination the bill to be constitutional. Permitting the attitude and practice of not being concerned about constitutionality of a bill by asserting that "it can be challenged later" is, without question, unconstitutional.

- It is unconstitutional for any executive to sign passed legislation into law without the executive reading, understanding, and determining the bill to be constitutional.

- It is unconstitutional to pass legislation and sign into law bills which subvert our Constitution as written.

- It is unconstitutional for the judiciary to make law by decisions made—decisions require instructions for legislatures to revise the law or strike down the law entirely. The courts have made law unconstitutionally but it is inherent upon the judiciary and especially the Supreme Court to render opinions and declarations in a way that does not create law.

- It is unconstitutional not to uphold, support, and defend our Constitution.

Observations and Assertions

Observations:

- Virtually every elected representative has not lived up to their "Oath of Office."
- Politics has perverted capitalism by creating the image of corruption by soliciting and receiving funds from other than individual constituents.
- With very few exceptions, the people I have discussed limiting campaign contributions to come only from constituents alone agree it is the right way.
- There is abundant proof that non-constituent donors affect the decision making of elected representatives.
- In over 60 years of eligibility no candidate has ever asked me for a contribution in person.
- Incumbents gain an advantage through a "Representational Relationship" established by accepting funds from Special Interests.

- Candidates in seeking contributions seek out higher contributions from other than individual constituents.
- With contributions comes invite, access and possible representation.
- A straight party vote often reveals a party as a Special Interest.
- Judicial decisions often reflect ideology influence.
- Legislation most often reflects some party influence.
- Administrative actions often reflect ideology influence.
- The interests of high donors has affected legislation, governance, litigation, adjudication, and law enforcement.
- Countless are the constitutional violations as some of the Campaign Finance Laws are not constitutional.
- Special Interest are all entities with an agenda seeking access, influence and representation who are not individual constituents.
- It is obvious that politicians including elected representatives often do not deliver on their promises.
- It is obvious politicians, representatives and political parties purposefully do not resolve certain issues as they use the issues like immigration as polarizing issues to motivate voters in an upcoming election(s).
- It is obvious that legislatures establish certain rules which upon the face are not democratic.
- It is obvious our founders created our "Form of Government" as being the "Representational Relationship" between duly elected representatives and their constituency.
- It is obvious that our "Form of Government" (the elected representing their constituents) has been ***ABRIDGED***.
- It is obvious the Representational Relationship (our "Form of Government") has not evolved as envisioned.
- It is obvious the attention of representatives is drawn towards the offerings of Special Interests and away from their constituency.

- It is obvious representative candidates focus on soliciting funds from Special Interests as they often provide more substantial funds than individual constituents.
- It is obvious that the political parties hold power and are the most influential and controlling Special Interest affecting our government.
- It is obvious representatives fall short in fulfilling their "Oath of Office."
- It is obvious representatives fall short in fulfilling their fiduciary duties.
- The injustice is in the creation of additional "Representational Relationships" by permitting other than individual constituents the means through which representation of constituents is diminished.
- Any attempt to justify the diminishing of the "Representational Relationship" lacks understanding of our Founders' Vision.
- It is obvious that the "Representational Relationships" between representatives and constituents are diminished whenever non-constituents and Special Interests gain more influence than constituents.
- It is obvious our "Form of Government" will cease to survive due to Campaign Finance Laws that political parties control.
- Our "Form of Government" is the "Representational Relationship" between duly elected representatives and their constituency.
- Special Interests include all other than individual constituents seeking to gain access and influence representatives in fulfilling the duties of the office being held.
- It is obvious the Executive Branch whose job is to enforce law selectively ignores enforcing certain laws. (Abraham Lin-

coln quote: "The best way to get a law repealed is to enforce it strictly.")

- It is obvious the legislatures ignore their "Oath of Office" to uphold, support, and defend our Constitution when they fail to assure passed legislation is constitutional.
- It is obvious the enforcement of laws lacks uniform enforcement by administrations.
- The Framers of our Constitution indicated their concern that the "Representational Relationship" needed to be fair.
- The "Representational Relationships" that have evolved are not fair as the "Representational Relationships" have diminished primarily as a result of the influence of campaign contributions producing additional "Representational Relationships."
- Candidate selection, especially for state and federal offices, has reflected the disproportionately influence of campaign contributions from non-constituents. Less than 10% of campaign contributions come from constituents.
- Money in politics has long been recognized as a major problem.
- Confidence ratings for Congress reflects the lack of effective fiduciary representation of constituents.
- Campaign Finance statutes have proven to diminish the "Representational Relationships" between representatives and constituents.
- Political parties have proven to be Special Interests as Campaign Finance Laws permit contributions which resulting in creating relationships which interfere with representatives from fulfilling fiduciary duties for constituents.
- Campaign Finance Laws provide advantages to incumbency to hold an office resulting in calls for creating term limits.
- Campaign Finance Laws provide advantages for parties to gain and hold power.

- Wealth, the elite and those holding power disproportionately influence all branches of government.
- Approval ratings of constituents of legislatures in particular are dismal reflecting a lack of quality "Representational Relationships."

ASSERTIONS:

- Our "Form of Government" is the "Representational Relationship" established between constituents and the elected representative as established through the electoral process.
- The established "Representational Relationships" (our "Form of Government") is supposed to be **sacrosanct**.
- Permitting interference with the established "Representational Relationships" interferes with our "Form of Government."
- Permitted interference diminishes the established relationship resulting in our "Form of Government" being "***ABRIDGED***."
- For our "Form of Government," to be and remain "***UN-ABRIDGED***," interference must not be permitted and be guarded against interference created through interpretations, executive actions, legislations, and adjudications.
- Representatives have a fiduciary responsibility with delegated authority to act on the behalf of constituents holding in trust their best interests.
- Our representatives in Congress have not acted in the best interest of their constituents and our nation as a whole as they have not shown fiscal responsibility allowing our notional debt to exceed 20 trillion dollars.

- Our representatives in Congress have not acted in the best interest of their constituents and our nation as a whole as they continually fail to produce a balanced budget which would hold accountable increases in our national debt.

- Our representatives in Congress do not act in the best interest of their constituents and our nation as a whole whenever they discard bipartisanship and fail to legislate in good faith.

- Political parties, politicians and elected representatives have evolved the campaign contribution laws and they appear to want the established structure to be maintained as it benefits them all.

- Contribution laws provides an advantage for incumbents as Special Interest representation created through contributions made and accepted becomes an automatic campaign funding source.

Recommendations

Following are recommendations our Democratic Republic needs:

- The House of Representatives and the Senate need to be active in understanding this perception I present and fulfill their fiduciary duty to revise Campaign Finance Laws as it is what the electorate desires and needs.
- All campaign laws need to be revised to limit campaign contributions to come only from individual citizens who are constituents.
- All campaign laws need to be revised to limit representative candidates and representatives to solicitation of and receiving campaign funds only from individual constituents.
- Constituents should vote only for candidates who live within the district they will represent.
- Constituents should vote only for candidates who fulfill their fiduciary duties, are honest, do not slander, defame, or libel.
- Constituents should vote for candidates who, when using personal funds, also solicit and accept funds from individual

constituents which portrays a welcomed dependency relationship with them.

Resulting Effect

after Recommendations Are Implemented

- Implementing recommendations will aid in saving our Democracy and Liberty.
- Incumbency will become more difficult to retain as the campaign funds will come from the same source as the playing field will be leveled to a high degree.
- More campaigns would depend upon "grass roots" support.
- Representative candidates and representatives will take on the image of being "untouchable" from Special Interests after implementation.
- Representatives will become more accountable to constituents by them improving their fiduciary compliance.
- More citizens will seek office.
- It will reduce corruption.
- Confidence in the representatives by constituents will improve dramatically by the improved "Representational Relationships."

Constitutional Challenge

Failure on the part of Congress to revise the Campaign Finance Laws has continually permitted Special Interests to maintain disproportional influence in government creating the need for a constitutional challenge to make its way to the Supreme Court (SCOTUS) for the Justices to make a determination as to the viability of this perception.

Any representative candidate or representative who has sought an elected office and has done so having followed the guidelines and recommendations put forth in this book and faced an opponent has not done the same has established standing and should consider filing suit that your constitutional rights have been violated.

I am *absolute* that the insights and perception I presented in this book are valid and I am confident our Supreme Court (SCOTUS) would, upon arguments, deliver a unanimous concurrence as to its constitutionality.